T0149300

PUT OFF / PUT ON

A Practical Application of Ephesians 4:17–32

JEFFREY E. STEPHENS

WESTBOW
P R E S S®
A DIVISION OF THOMAS NELSON
& ZONDERVAN

WestBow Press books may be ordered through booksellers or by contacting:

WestBow Press
A Division of Thomas Nelson & Zondervan
1663 Liberty Drive
Bloomington, IN 47403
www.westbowpress.com
1 (866) 928-1240

ISBN: 978-1-9736-1915-4 (sc)
ISBN: 978-1-9736-1916-1 (e)

Library of Congress Control Number: 2018901612

Print information available on the last page.

WestBow Press rev. date: 02/13/2018

Acknowledgements

I want to take a moment to recognize those who have had a hand in the development of this short book. The first recognition goes to the Lord Jesus Christ. Without Him, I am nothing, and because of Him, there has been drastic change in my own life. I thank Him most of all.

My wife, Sharon, is also due many thanks. She has been my partner for over forty years and seen my dark side. She has read this book and made many suggestions that I have followed.

In addition, untold and unnamed others have contributed to this book by influencing my life in the academic and professional world. It would be impossible to give credit to every individual or book that has impacted my life, bringing me to the place I am today.

My understanding of how spiritual growth works can be contributed mainly to Dr. Jay Adams and his books, *Competent to Counsel* and *The Christian Counselor's Manual*. I am certain many more authors deserve recognition. Many thanks to their willingness to share their knowledge with me through the milieu of the written word.

Introduction

It happened again. A middle-aged man who wanted to be saved approached me after a Sunday morning service. Ordinarily this would excite me, but now it was frustrating me. I had previously spoken to this man about his salvation. We spent a couple hours going over what salvation is, how it is received, and what is to happen next. He went away confident of his salvation, or so I thought. Now he was back.

This time I asked him, "Didn't you get saved before?"

He answered, "Yes! I got saved five times yesterday."

In my subsequent discussion with him, he indicated he wanted to make sure he was truly saved. I discovered that he wanted to be saved again because he did not feel saved. His life was not living up to the expectations he had set for himself regarding how a believer should live. Hence, he thought, if he were truly saved, he would be living up to those anticipations.

As a pastor, I often encounter people who have been saved multiple times. In each case, it appears the person does not understand that salvation is not a feeling. This individual has not yet understood the need to live a changed life. The person thinks his or her old way of living will just go away and he or she will automatically have a better life and have no more struggles with sinful habits.

In reality, these people have not learned that the Christian life is a process of growth that occurs on a steady incline toward Christ-likeness, but also has its ups and downs as they succeed more often in overcoming their sin. It is akin to walking up a sand dune on Lake Michigan. You dig in with your feet, but because of the squishiness of the sand, you don't make much progress. It is like taking two steps forward and one step backward.

Like most of us, this man thinks spiritual growth is something that just happens as you live out your life, but this is a false notion. A brief reading of the apostle Paul's letters reveals the nature of spiritual growth is more akin to the training of an athlete or soldier or the discipline of a farmer. These metaphors make it clear that, in spiritual growth, there is need for patience, discipline, training, and hard work in developing one's character and practice in the Christian life.

This man did not need to be saved again, so far as I could tell. What he needed was to learn the process of growth.

I am convinced from my own experience that most believers are not taught how to grow spiritually. In fact, I think if you ask the average believer how to grow spiritually, his or her answer would look something like this, "Pray, read your Bible, attend church, be baptized, give your tithes and offerings, and get involved in the church."

These are good and right to do, but they will not be enough for spiritual growth. These same people probably could not outline the process of spiritual growth as Scripture portrays it. Nor could they tell you what area of their lives they most need to grow in. They somehow have the idea that spiritual growth occurs through osmosis.

Spiritual growth is more specific and intentional than that. It deals with transforming a drug addict into a self-controlled sober person, a liar into a truth-teller, or an abusive man into a gentle individual. The kind of transformation the Bible talks about takes more than just reading about change in the Bible and attending church. It takes the exercise of certain principles in daily life.

John,[1] a friend I met in a Bible study at our county jail, is an example of a changed man. In a recent letter, he said he was a selfish, proud, egotistical man; however, God had transformed him. Here is how that change became evident in his life.

He had been given the opportunity to be an assistant pastor in the prison church. After much prayer and review of 2 Timothy 3–4, he turned it down. He did not want to lead the church in the wrong direction. He really wanted the position and loved to speak the Word to others, but if he would have taken the position, it would have been at the expense of another man who had been around longer and deserved the honor as well. How did John go from the selfish man he was to the generous, self-sacrificing man he is today? That is what this book is all about.

I think an explanation of the change John made is an essential part of spiritual growth. Therefore, I am astounded to see the shelves of our Christian bookstores lined with dozens of books on spiritual growth, yet I have not seen one that plainly discusses Paul's teaching on the subject of the

---

[1] All names have been changed to protect their identity.

put-off-and-put-on process as found in Ephesians 4:17–32. Serious believers want to grow spiritually, but they do not even know that a distinct process is laid out in Scripture. They do not have to invent the wheel all over again. The process is there for the using and growing.

I intend this book to be a discoverer's guide to growing spiritually. It is an interactive influence that will call you to examine your life in order to determine what areas of your life you most need to grow in. Then it will show you from Scripture how to grow in that area to be more like Christ.

CHAPTER ONE

Sin City

Before we can gain an understanding of the meaning of Ephesians 4, we need to take a peek into life in Ephesus so we can better understand the dynamics of the people Paul was writing to. This will help us to recognize the similarities in our own lives and enable us to grasp truths Paul intends us to practice in our lives today.

Ephesus was a major commercial city of the Roman Empire in Asia, maintaining a population of 330,000. The city flaunted its wealth and commerce. A theater built into Mt. Pion had a seating capacity of 25,000, and a stadium held a 24,000-seat capacity. It was a cosmopolitan city that was tolerant of religion for the most part. According to the New Bible Dictionary, "It became a centre of the emperor cult, and eventually possessed three official temples, thus qualifying thrice over for the proud title *ne_okoros* ('temple-warden') of the emperors, as well as being *ne_okoros* of Artemis (Acts 19:35)."[2]

If entertainment were what you sought, ample sporting events were held in its stadium, everything from gladiator games to chariot racing and reenactments of past battles. Needless to say, the city was a cesspool of every known vice. A modern-day counterpart might be the likes of Chicago, Los Angeles, or even a Midwest city like Grand Rapids, Michigan.

When Paul arrived with Aquilla and Priscilla (Acts 18:19–21), he found a city that was desperately in need of a true spiritual awakening. He spent some time teaching in the synagogue and must have had some converts there who desired him to stay with them for awhile. He refused the invitation in order to continue on his trip to Jerusalem. Later he returned and spent two years (Acts 19:1–20:1) in Ephesus, teaching the believers and building them into a church.

Here in Ephesus, the silversmiths dragged Paul into the stadium. The silversmiths manufactured and marketed statues of the goddess Diana. Soon after Paul cast a demon out of a young woman who was the face of their company, they began to lose revenue. They blamed Paul and dragged him into the stadium in order to exact their revenge.

The citizens of Ephesus, many of whom became believers, would have brought every type of sinful habit imaginable into their Christian life, just as people do today.

---

[2] D. R. W. Wood and I. H. Marshall, *New Bible Dictionary*, 3rd ed. (Leicester, England; Downers Grove, Ill.: InterVarsity Press, 1996), 327.

Thus Paul's instructions on how to deal with those habits is relevant to today.

These people were just as dead as the silver gods they worshiped. They were "dead in trespasses and sins" (Eph. 2:1). They had been pursuing an elusive dream of satisfaction, empty promises of happiness, and the good life, only to be set back by the emptiness they felt after a tryst with the temple prostitute or the failed restoration of health after a trip to the local spa. Life was just as empty, dull, and hard as it is today for anyone who seeks peace in things that cannot produce it. I am sure, if anyone of us could travel back in time and be jettisoned onto the streets of Ephesus, save for our clothing and a few other technologies, we would fit right in, insofar as we are pursuing the same things they did.

But Paul has good news for them and us. Life does not have to be one empty bottle or relationship after another. It can be different. Paul makes it quite clear to the believer that we were dead. We were following one lust after another. But that is just the point. We were. We are not now, or at least we aren't supposed to be.

I read recently of an elderly woman who lived the life of a bag lady. She lived in a dumpy house, wore ragged clothes, and ate garbage. When she died, the police found almost a half-million dollars stashed around her house. She lived like a homeless person, but she did not have to. Do you live today like that bag lady, eating the garbage of society, clothed in rags that show your class rather than the robes of purity and peace? The trouble with most believers is they have not a clue that they have the power and resources to overcome the habits that keep them in bondage right inside them and in their Bibles.

CHAPTER TWO

When Anger Gets the Upper Hand

Joe was playing canasta with his wife, Debbie, the other day. She grew up playing cards, and when she was around her mother or sisters, they always got in a game of pinochle. Recently while on vacation with her sister and brother-in-law, they learned to play canasta, commonly called hand and foot. They had so much fun that he made a commitment with himself to play cards with her every day (when possible) so he could spend time doing something with her that she absolutely enjoyed. He was being the good husband.

Debbie was a sharp player. Joe knew this, and he was resigned to losing most of the time. Or so he thought. Joe, a very competitive guy, could be a sore loser. He hated to lose at anything. Because he was such a sore loser, he avoided playing games because of what it brought out in him. But he thought he would do this for Debbie. Well, losing was what Joe did when he played against Debbie. It finally came to a head on the day in question.

One day when he lost, he thought that things were going pretty well for him during the game. It was the end of the first of four hands when Debbie unexpectedly went out on him, causing him to lose points, he lost it. He slammed his fist down on the portable table, mixed up the cards, and quit. He realized he needed help. The help Joe needed to control his anger is what I am about to tell you.

Paul said in Ephesians 4:22–24, "That ye put off concerning the former conversation the old man, which is corrupt according to the deceitful lusts; And be renewed in the spirit of your mind; And that ye put on the new man, which after God is created in righteousness and true holiness."

The process is right here. Simply put, it involves putting off the old man (the sinful habits like anger or lying) and putting on the new man (habits of righteousness like self-control, love, truth-telling, and so on). But there is much more to that set of instructions than meets the eye. We will explore this process of putting off the old man and putting on the new man in the next chapter.

CHAPTER THREE

Put Off the Old Man

On the Surface

I am making an assumption here that you, the reader, are a believer in Jesus Christ. This is important for several reasons:

1. Paul is writing to believers at Ephesus, "Paul, an apostle of Jesus Christ by the will of God to the *saints* (emphasis added) which are at Ephesus and to the *faithful* in Christ Jesus" (Eph. 1:1). He is not, therefore, giving unbelievers a way to grow and change. Such thinking would not even occur to apostle Paul. In fact, he would say that would not even be possible.

2. Paul, citing the psalms in Romans 3:10–18, reminds us that unbelievers cannot follow this process with success. Nor would they want to. Furthermore, he states in 1 Corinthians 2:14, "The natural man

receiveth not the things of the Spirit of God: for they are foolishness unto him: neither can he know them, because they are spiritually discerned." To Paul, the "natural man" is an unbeliever. Paul clearly sets forth that an unbeliever cannot do what he is calling believers to do in putting off the old man.

You might be reading this because someone has given this booklet to you due to the fact that you are struggling with some problem in your life. As stated above, if you are not a believer, you cannot do what Paul is instructing you to do. Therefore, you will not be able to experience the change and the peace that comes with that transformation in your personal thinking and habits. At this point, let me explain how to become a believer.

An Aside

Maybe someone has given you this book because he or she recognizes you need a change in your life. However, you may not be a believer. So let me take a few lines and share with you how you can know that you are a true believer in Jesus Christ.

As stated earlier, you will not be able to succeed in this change if you do not know Jesus Christ as your Savior. Here is how you can know. First, you must recognize that you have a problem. You are a sinner. The Bible says, "For all have sinned and come short of the glory of God" (Rom. 3:23). It also states, "There is none righteous, no not one: there is none that understandeth, there is none that seeketh after God" (Rom. 3:10–11). We are all sinners. You are a sinner, and the "wages of sin is death" (Rom. 6:23).

God has a remedy in Jesus Christ. "While we were yet sinners Christ died for us" (Rom. 5:8). He also stated, "The wages of sin is death, the gift of God is eternal life through Jesus Christ our Lord" (Rom. 6:23). So then, God has provided a payment for our sin that we could not pay. That was the death of Jesus on the cross. Then Paul stated in Romans 10:9–13, "That if thou shalt confess with thy mouth the Lord Jesus and believe in thine heart that God hath raised him from the dead thou shalt be saved … for whosoever shall call upon the name of the Lord shall be saved."

In short, if you acknowledge that you are a sinner worthy of death and you repent of your sin and call upon Jesus to save you, God will save you. Now is the day of salvation if you have not already put your trust in Him. Just say a prayer like this—in your own words of course—and mean it in your heart. "Lord Jesus, I know I am a sinner. I ask you to forgive me of my sin and come into my heart and save me. In Jesus' name, amen." Having done that, now you can go on to see change in your life.

Having said that, the first step to putting off the old man is to discover which part of that old man needs to be removed. Now most of us can probably put our finger on one or two habits we have that we know are wrong, like Joe's anger issue.

Anger is not always an issue with Joe. On occasion, he can sit down and play cards with his wife and have no problem, even if he loses. But anger, like a lot of other issues in life, might just reside under the surface, only to appear when it unexpectedly lets loose.

If you are reading this book, you already know you have a problem with some area in your life. That is why you are reading this. So take that problem and identify it in biblical terms. This is one important step because the terms we often use for sinful habits today are not often found in Scripture.

An example is that of alcoholism. The word "alcoholic" is not found in Scripture. However, the term "drunk" or "drunkenness" is. So once you identify what you know to be the sin you need to put off, then it is time to find the verse that deals with that issue. Any good topical index of the Bible will help you to find those passages.

The text we are using highlights a few habitual sins as examples or case studies for us to chew on. Notice that Paul addressed the issue of lying in Ephesians 4:25, "Wherefore putting away lying, speak every man truth with his neighbor: for we are members one of another."

You may not have an issue with lying. No matter what your issue is, the process will be the same. Paul simply identifies lying as the issue at hand to be dealt with. Now a person who has a habit of telling bald-faced lies obviously has a problem, but lying can take many forms. People lie in many ways. When you understand this, you just might change your evaluation of self as not being a liar.

Lying is any form of untruth. For example, it can take the form of exaggeration. When we use words like "never" or "always" in a conversation, we most likely are not speaking accurately. When our tone of voice or body language does not match what we are saying, we are knee-deep in deception. When we "beat around the bush," as we say, rather than speaking what we mean, we are involved in deception. In this case, we are hoping that the person we are speaking to catches what we mean. It is an attempt on our part to be softer or to not look like the bad guy.

For example, a wife says to her husband, "Honey, I left my purse in the car."

That is most likely not a statement meant for simple conversation. She left out an important part, which will show up when her husband does not move from his chair to retrieve her purse.

What she really meant was, "Honey, I left my purse in the car. Would you get it for me?"

She says it this way because speaking the truth right out might get her a snide remark in return. She is trying to protect herself from disappointment. This kind of communication, more than likely, happens much of the time. Thus, the first step is to recognize what you need to put off.

Up to this point, I have only been speaking of sinful habits that are on the surface. They are behaviors that are clearly seen by the eye and heard by the ear. I call these "surface issues" because they are on the surface of daily life. They are the visible manifestations of our sin. Joe's anger was visible when he threw the cards in the earlier illustration. These are mere symptoms of the deeper problem, which I call under-the-surface issues. We will deal with them a little later. But for now, just remember that you are going to have to work on two levels: the surface level (symptom) and the under-the-surface level (root problem). It is necessary to uncover both levels in order to affect true change in your life.

Not only do you need to know what sinful habit to put

off, you also need to know when you habitually practice your sin. This is important because sinful habits have a way of masquerading as other things in different parts of life. This is like a weed in a garden. It is not enough to simply jerk out the weed or cut it off at ground level. Weeds have roots, and they spread all over the garden, not just in one area. So it is with sinful habits. They will occur with your spouse and children. These habits will crop up at work or at play. You need to know when and where this sinful practice occurs so you can take steps to avoid it.

I was driving my car one day, and I came up over a hill and hit a deep pothole. It threw the alignment off in my steering. I had to pay hard-earned cash to have the alignment straightened out in my car. From that point on, I knew the pothole was there and veered to the right just enough to miss that rut every time I drove over that stretch of road. This is why it is necessary to discover when and where your sin occurs in your life. Sinful habits are like the pothole. Sin events do not just happen. They occur at specific times when we are set up for the fall.

A man has a lust problem, which comes up when he watches sports on TV and the cheerleaders are shown. When he goes shopping with his wife at the mall, he knows those are places where he might fail. If he knows this, he can take steps to avoid the failure.

The question is: how do you find this out? That is an excellent question that anyone wanting to put off the old man must answer. The tool I use for discovery is a journal. I use the journal in the following way when there has been a failure or the practice of a sinful habit. There are four questions to answer. (These are also in Appendix A for you to copy).

1. What happened?
   a. *Write down information describing the situation that led to the failure. The key is to not try to write down everything, but enough so you can recall what happened.*
2. What did I do?
   a. *What was my response to what happened? This would describe the sin. For example, "Joe threw his cards off the table."*
3. What should I have done in response to what happened?
   a. *This answers: what did God want me to do? Of course the answer comes from the Scripture.*
4. What do I need to do now? What does the Scripture say I need to do to correct the situation?
   a. *These questions come from the "Problem Solution Sheet" (page 311) found in Jay Adam's book, The Christian Counselor's Manual.*

I was describing this process to a group of men during a Bible study at the county jail when a man named Tom piped up and asked if he could make a comment.

I said, "Sure."

Tom proceeded to describe that he had a foul mouth and the Lord had convinced him that it was not right. He needed to change. He began to make a tick-mark on a letter-sized sheet of paper every time he swore. He said he filled both sides of the paper the first few days. (This was a week later that he was telling us this story.) He showed me his paper for that day, and it only had a few tick-marks on it. He had made drastic progress. This is what I am talking about. He kept track, and in doing so, he found his potholes and took steps to avoid them.

Let me use Tom's example of a foul mouth to show you how this would look. For every tick-mark, Tom would write down what happened that led him to swear. It could be that he was around a group of guys playing cards and he lost the hand. He would swear, as this was his habit. This answers questions one and two, what happened and what he did.

Once Tom had these questions answered, he would need to determine what he should have done. He had some options. He might have just kept his mouth closed and said nothing. He could have replaced the swear word with a word of praise for the other guy's playing skill. This would be based on Ephesians 4:29 in our text, "Let no corrupt communication proceed out of your mouth, but that which is good for the use of edifying that it may minister grace to the hearers."

Finally, what he should do now? He should ask forgiveness from God and those around him who heard it. 1 John 1:9 says, "If we confess our sins, he is faithful and just to forgive us our sins and cleanse us from all unrighteousness." (See also Matthew 5:3–26).

As Tom follows this process of discovery over the course of a week or two, he will be able to see the patterns, those potholes that trip him up. And once he sees the array, he will then be better equipped to take steps to control himself and handle the situation in a manner that pleases God. So it is with us.

If you know you have a sinful habit in your life and God leads you to put it off, then keep a journal with enough information that you can discover how often you fail in that area and when. Use these questions as a format for discovery. Then you can begin to mortify the sin, as Paul told us to in Romans 8:13, "For if ye live after the flesh, ye shall die; but if ye through the Spirit do mortify the deeds of the body, ye shall live."

Now you know what you need to put off, determine what part of the old man needs to go. You also know how deeply rooted it is in your life and when you are most likely to default to that pattern of behavior.

Under the Surface

As I mentioned earlier, it is crucial for you to get at the root cause of your sinful habit. Remember the weed illustration I used earlier? Let's take another look at that. The weed you see above the ground simply lets you know you have weeds in your garden. If all you do is pluck them off, you have not solved your weed problem. The root is still growing underground and will pop up again in your garden. In order to eradicate the weed problem, you must get rid of the root. Until that happens, you will still have your weed problem. It is the same spiritually. In the analogy, simply replace the word "weed" with the word "sin," and you see what I mean.

In my card-playing illustration, the problem was not Joe throwing the cards … although it was part of the issue. It was the visible weed, but it was not the real problem. He needs to get at the root cause of "Why did he throw the cards?" This is the under-the-surface issue. The Bible calls these idols. I call them the "idol of the heart."

The idol of Joe's heart drove him to throw the cards when Debbie won the hand. You understand that throwing the cards was just a symptom of the problem. It is the surface issue that reveals there is a deeper problem, a root sin. It is like the red light on the dashboard of your car. When it comes on, you know something is wrong. The light tells you to check the engine. It implies you will do so before the problem gets worse and you have to replace the engine, which will be very costly. The question is: how do you get to the root of the problem? That is where a second set of questions that sound very similar to the first four enter the picture.

The following questions will help you to discover the root issue of your sinful habit. (These are also in Appendix B for you to copy)

1. What happened?
2. What was I wanting when the event happened?
3. What does the Bible say about what I was wanting?
4. What do I need to do now?

What Happened?

Like the first set of questions, this merely records the circumstances surrounding the sinful conduct.

Jeffrey E. Stephens

What Was I Wanting When the Event Happened?

This is slightly different than the second question in the first set. The aim of this question is to uncover the inner motive or desire that precipitated the response. In the first set of questions, it was, "What did I do?" This question gets at what I was wanting so bad that, when that event happened, I was willing to sin against God (and the other person) in order to get it. This is the root of the matter, the motive behind the way you responded. It is actually what Jesus was referring to in Matthew 15:19 when he spoke about what comes out of the mouth first comes from the thoughts. "For out of the heart proceed evil thoughts, murders, adulteries, fornications, thefts, false witness, blasphemies."

The heart or thinking of a person drives what he or she does. In short, you do what you do because you think what you think. Or you do what you do because you want what you want. To apply this question to your situation is a crucial step in discovering the idol of your heart.

In going back to my illustration of throwing the cards, what do you think Joe was wanting? What was the idol of his heart? You might answer, "To win." You would be correct, but it goes deeper than that. It was really a pride issue. Joe didn't want to fall short, or to put it another way, Joe wanted the preeminence. Joe wanted to be first. Joe wanted to be thought of or proven to be smarter, sharper, and more capable than his wife. Instead he appeared stupid or less than her, and he didn't like that.

Now this idol of the heart is not going to show up in his life just in playing a card game. Not at all. It will show up in all areas of life. Like the weed that shows up in the garden, the root of it is growing underneath the entire garden, not just part of it.

Remember the "bonk" game in the arcade where funny heads pop up out of a hole and you have to bonk it before it goes back down? When you bonk one head, another pops up out of one of the other nine holes. The idols of your heart show up in all areas of your life, like the heads that pop up in different holes in the bonk game. You bonk the lie here, the off-color word there, and then the angry outburst over here, and you just keep bonking.

But if you just pull out the guts from underneath the surface, you kill the entire scheme and no longer wear yourself out while trying to bonk each sin. You have unplugged the power behind the sin, so to speak. You have pulled out the root and killed it so the weed no longer grows.

What Does the Bible Say about What Joe Was Wanting?

This question piggybacks off question two. Notice that we are still speaking of idols. What was Joe wanting when he sinned? The Bible speaks of putting off the root causes of sin. Once you identify the root cause, you are ready to call it what the Bible calls it. John refers to some of these causes in 1 John 2:16, "The lust of the flesh, and the lust of the eyes, and the pride of life." These three generally cover all of the idols of the heart. In 3 John 9, John gives us an example of a man whose idol of the heart is the love of preeminence. "But

Diotrophes, who loveth to have the preeminence among them, receiveth us not."

If you read the passage, you discover that his idolatrous love of preeminence led him to hinder the work of others in the church where he was. He wouldn't receive strangers or travelers into the church, not even John himself. This man clearly had a pride problem.

You might further understand the idols of the heart as those things you think you have a right to, for example, a right to privacy, rest, respect, control of your life, trouble free life, and so on. When you figure out what the Bible says about what you wanted, that is, identifying it as sin, then you are ready to figure out what you need to do now. That leads us to the last question.

What Do I Need to Do Now?

This leads you to recovery. Three different passages can help us here.

> Therefore if thou bring thy gift to the altar, and there rememberest that thy brother hath ought against thee; Leave there thy gift before the altar, and go thy way; first be reconciled to thy brother, and then come and offer thy gift. Agree with thine adversary quickly, whiles thou art in the way with him; lest at any time the adversary deliver thee to the judge, and the judge deliver thee to the officer, and thou be cast into prison. Verily I say unto thee,

Thou shalt by no means come out thence,
till thou hast paid the uttermost farthing
(Matt. 5:23–26).

Moreover if thy brother shall trespass
against thee, go and tell him his fault
between thee and him alone: if he shall
hear thee, thou hast gained thy brother.
But if he will not hear thee, then take with
thee one or two more, that in the mouth
of two or three witnesses every word may
be established. And if he shall neglect to
hear them, tell it unto the church: but if he
neglect to hear the church, let him be unto
thee as an heathen man and a publican.
Verily I say unto you, Whatsoever ye shall
bind on earth shall be bound in heaven:
and whatsoever ye shall loose on earth shall
be loosed in heaven. Again I say unto you,
That if two of you shall agree on earth as
touching any thing that they shall ask, it
shall be done for them of my Father which
is in heaven. For where two or three are
gathered together in my name, there am I
in the midst of them (Matt. 18:15–20).

If we confess our sins he is faithful and just
to forgive us our sins and cleanse us from
all unrighteousness (1 John 1:9).

These passages deal with getting things right with others
and God in terms of our sin. The first passage speaks of

dealing with our own sin by confessing and repenting of it and then going to the offended person to ask forgiveness. The second passage deals with our going to someone who has sinned against us and helping him or her make it right. The third passage deals with our own confession of sin to God.

We have now figured out what we need to put off. We have seen how to put that sin off. Now we need to address the second step, which has to do with changing our thinking. That is what the next chapter is about.

CHAPTER FOUR

Changing Your Thinking

The second step in the put-off-and-put-on process is found in verse 23, "and be renewed in the spirit of your mind."

What Is Renewal?

In order to understand what Paul meant here, we need to examine a few of the words he chose to use. The word "be renewed" means "to make new or renew" (Theological Dictionary of the New Testament, *ananeoo)*. This is not to be understood in the way of simply taking the old and splashing a coat of paint on it though. It is rather referring to making something new in such a way that the old is not recognizable. It is not restoring something old to its original, like new condition, as in restoring or renewing a vintage automobile. No, not at all. This would be more like taking the parts of that vintage automobile and making a boat out of it. It is that radical. They are the same parts, but unrecognizable as to their former use.

This is also not self-renewal. Grammatically, the word is a passive infinitive as in "to be," but is acting like an imperative. In other words, the word is translated "to be renewed," but it's intention is more of a command. It is not a suggestion. It has a forcefulness behind it. Yet the action of the verb means that this renewal is something that is done to the believer, not something the believer does.

In other words, you don't renew yourself. We also see this renewal is to occur in the mind, as our text states. The mind, as Paul meant it, is our inner thinking, the inner man. It is what Paul had in mind when he stated in Philippians 2:2, "Fulfil ye my joy, that ye be likeminded, having the same love, being of one accord, of one mind." And verse 5 states, "Let this mind be in you which is also in Christ Jesus." It represents a complete change in thinking and subsequently a complete alteration in behavior. So the location of the transformation or renewing is identified as the "spirit of your mind."

What does this mean to us? What does it look like in real life? Because this renewal of the mind is something that is not done by us, but is accomplished in us, what is our responsibility to affect this? Let me illustrate first the concept of renewing as meant in our text.

I once held a church service at the county jail. All participating in the service were in one particular room along with the inmates. Years later, I was at the same county jail holding a Bible study. The room we were in seemed to be in the same general vicinity as the area I mentioned formerly.

I found out later that, in fact, it was the same room,

but had been completely renovated, changing the size and appearance so it was unrecognizable. Doors were moved, and the shape of the room was altered. I knew I was in the same place, but I wasn't sure until I asked.

Now then, it is the same with the renewal of the mind. The believer is the same person—as far as appearances— that they were before they became a believer. Nevertheless, what occurs on the inside of a man is bound to change his outward appearance to some degree. It won't alter the color of the eyes or stature, but it might change his or her joy, which will most certainly show up in his or her countenance. What then is the process of renewal?

Setting Yourself Up for Renewal

The process of renewal is passive. Let me illustrate it this way. Let's say a young man goes to school to be an auto mechanic. (You can fill in the blank with anything really.) He attends classes, works on engines, and so on, and he even gets a degree. This doesn't mean he is a mechanic. It just means he knows how to do mechanic work. When he gets a job or begins working on engines, then he has become a mechanic. He could get the degree but not actually work in that field. In fact, he might work in that field but not really be a mechanic. He could be like a fish out of water or simply masquerading as a mechanic. In other words, in order for him to be a mechanic, he has to put everything in place from his training and education. He has worked on engines, and over time, he has become known as a mechanic. He who once was not a mechanic is now a mechanic.

Let me give you another illustration. Let's say a man,

Jeffrey E. Stephens

who is a husband and father and also has a severe anger problem, becomes a believer. He begins to read and study the Scripture and to apply the truths he learns to his life. He, the Bible states, has become a new creation (2 Cor. 5:17) when he puts his faith in Jesus Christ. However, that newness has come about by the work of the Holy Spirit.

Let's say he begins to memorize and apply verses that pertain to his situation, for example, Philippians 2:3–4, "Let nothing be done through strife or vainglory; but in lowliness of mind let each esteem other better than themselves. Look not every man on his own things, but every man also on the things of others."

As he applies the verses to his situation when he finds himself beginning to become angry, he discovers that his thinking is changing. Rather than putting himself first, as was his habit, he begins to put others first. It is not that he is changing his thinking, but the Spirit of God is using the Word of God to change his thinking. The Holy Spirit takes him from being an angry person to a self-controlled person.

Now then, let us say that some of his friends haven't seen him in awhile. They knew him as an angry, selfish person. When they see him again, he looks like the same guy who was their friend, but they notice a difference in the way he conducts his life. Instead of that selfish, angry person they once knew, he is now a kind and generous person. They can hardly believe the transformation. That is what Paul meant by being "renewed in the spirit of your mind."

Thus, as a person reads and studies the Scripture and begins to apply the truths to his or her life, this person's thinking begins to change in an almost unnoticeable way. And as this individual's thinking begins to change, so does his or her conduct. And as this person's conduct changes, so does his or her feelings/emotions.

A Few Biblical Illustrations

Take, for instance, that man with an unclean spirit recorded in Mark 5.

> And they came over unto the other side of the sea, into the country of the Gadarenes. And when he was come out of the ship, immediately there met him out of the tombs a man with an unclean spirit, Who had his dwelling among the tombs; and no man could bind him, no, not with chains: Because that he had been often bound with fetters and chains, and the chains had been plucked asunder by him, and the fetters broken in pieces: neither could any man tame him. And always, night and day, he was in the mountains, and in the tombs, crying, and cutting himself with stones. But when he saw Jesus afar off, he ran and worshipped him, And cried with a loud voice, and said, What have I to do with thee, Jesus, thou Son of the most high God? I adjure thee by God, that thou torment me not. For he said unto him, Come out of the man, thou unclean spirit. And he asked him, What is thy name? And he answered, saying, My name is Legion: for we are many.

> And he besought him much that he would not send them away out of the country. Now there was there nigh unto the mountains a great herd of swine feeding. And all the devils besought him, saying, Send us into the swine, that we may enter into them. And forthwith Jesus gave them leave. And the unclean spirits went out, and entered into the swine: and the herd ran violently down a steep place into the sea, (they were about two thousand;) and were choked in the sea. And they that fed the swine fled, and told it in the city, and in the country. And they went out to see what it was that was done. And they come to Jesus, and see him that was possessed with the devil, and had the legion, sitting, and clothed, and in his right mind: and they were afraid.

Notice the man with the unclean spirit, whom no one could bind. Nothing could hold him secure. He was always crying and cutting himself with stones. After Jesus commanded the unclean spirit to leave him, that same man was seen sitting calmly and in his right mind, whereas before nothing could make him sit. He was clothed, whereas before no garments stayed on him. He was in his right mind, whereas before he was out of his mind. The man was the same man, but an encounter with Jesus Christ had renewed him.

How about the man born blind whom Jesus gave sight? After the man was given his sight, the people who knew him said, "The neighbours therefore, and they which before had seen him that he was blind, said, Is not this he that sat and begged? Some said, This is he: others said, He is like him: but he said, I am he" (John 9:8–9).

Here again we have a man who was blind and forced to beg. He had always been known as a blind beggar. Now after his encounter with Jesus, he was no longer blind. He had been renewed. He was so different that those who were his neighbors—those who had known him all his life and those who had grown so accustomed to seeing him begging on the street—no longer noticed him. Now they were not even sure he was the same person.

One final example of the drastic change called renewal that happens to a person who encounters Jesus was seen in Zaccheus, a tax collector by profession. He was a man of short stature, but one who obviously was one of considerable importance. He put himself in the right place when he heard Jesus was coming through. What happened next has been made popular in children's Bible storybooks and Bible songs and is worth taking a look at. Luke 19 gives us the record.

> And Jesus entered and passed through Jericho. And, behold, there was a man named Zacchaeus, which was the chief among the publicans, and he was rich. And he sought to see Jesus who he was; and could not for the press, because he was little of stature. And he ran before, and climbed up into a sycamore tree to see him: for he was to pass that way. And when Jesus came to the place, he looked up, and saw him,

> and said unto him, Zacchaeus, make haste, and come down; for today I must abide at thy house. And he made haste, and came down, and received him joyfully. And when they saw it, they all murmured, saying, That he was gone to be guest with a man that is a sinner. And Zacchaeus stood, and said unto the Lord; Behold, Lord, the half of my goods I give to the poor; and if I have taken any thing from any man by false accusation, I restore him fourfold.

Zaccheus sought to see Jesus so he ran ahead on his route. He climbed a tree so he could get a glimpse of Him as He passed by. Jesus saw him, and the rest is history. Notice the change in him however. He said, "Behold, Lord, the half of my goods I give to the poor; and if I have taken anything from any man by false accusation, I restore him fourfold."

Now can you imagine what those who knew him would be saying after hearing that? They knew him as a greedy little man, one who was probably stingy with his things as well as his money. But now that he had encountered Jesus, he was a renewed man.

Renewing Your Mind

Now I hope you are getting the idea of what it means to be renewed in the spirit of your mind. To be renewed, you must set yourself up for renewal. If you want to be just as radically changed as the men in our illustration, you have to set yourself up for that change. You have begun the process because you have put your faith in Jesus Christ. You have recognized the habitual sin(s) that you must put off (the old man). You have to set yourself up for success here. You must read the Word, obey the commands you discover, pray for wisdom and understanding, get counsel from those who have already successfully navigated the path you are going down, memorize relevant Scripture passages and think through them, and then apply them to your life situation.

Let's say you are struggling just now with anger. You find yourself driving down the road, and someone pulls out in front of you, driving slowly. You would normally blast your horn, shake your fist at the driver, zoom by the person, and give him or her a dirty look or worse.

However, this time you apply these first two principles to the situation. You say to yourself, "I am not going to be mad at this person. This individual has as much right to the road as I do. God is in control of this situation, and He must want me to slow down."

Along with this self-talk, you remember your memory verse, Proverbs 14:29, "He that is slow to wrath is of great understanding: but he that is hasty of spirit exalteth folly." Your response then is to slow down and relax. The more you make this your practice, the more you will find that soon you don't even get angry when someone pulls out in front of you and drives slowly. You have been renewed in your mind. You have set yourself up for the Holy Spirit to renew you. You have become a changed man.

However, the text that is our object of study does not stop with putting off the old man and being renewed in the spirit of your mind. No, it continues to the third step, the object of the next chapter.

CHAPTER FIVE

Putting On the New Man

Our text says, "And that ye put on the new man, which after God is created in righteousness and true holiness" (Eph. 4:24). So you know you have to put off your anger (or whatever your sinful habit is) and set yourself up to be renewed in your mind. Once those are in place, then you have to replace the sinful anger, like yelling or hitting something or someone with its opposite. That is the subject of this chapter.

We must now discover what the opposite of anger, bitterness, lust, pride, and so on is and begin to practice that when we are tempted to be like our old man. We need to answer a few questions from our text before we can figure those out though.

First, what is meant by the phrase, "which after God"? Then what did Paul mean when he said "created in righteousness and true holiness"? Once we answer those questions, we will be ready to discover what the opposites are of our particular sinful habit.

The word "after" is a word in the Greek that means "according to." In this case, its reference is God. So we could say that Paul meant that the new man was going to be like God in character or conduct. The new man was according to the pattern of God. So Paul was speaking of a believer who was dominated by the divine nature. Whereas the old man was dominated by the fleshly nature, now the believer was to be dominated by God's mind. This new man, as he described it, was not new in time, but in quality. It was "created in righteousness and true holiness," which further explained the divine nature. In short, the new man is to replace the sinful habits or conduct of the old man with the righteous and holy habits of the new man.

Thus, an angry man would put off the sinful habits that are demonstrated by the yelling or screaming or how they are manifested in his life and instead put on self-control that would look like controlling his words and tone of voice. We have already seen that this also has to be done on the inner-man level, the level of the mind or thinking. The idol of the heart that drives the anger also has to be put off and replaced with its righteous counterpart. Hence, if one's anger is driven by a desire to have peace and quiet by yelling at the kids to leave you alone, the opposite of that would be to find peace in God, not in one's circumstances.

As you can see, this step is finding out what God would want you to think and do or say in response to the event that triggers the sin and then obeying. The tool that helps with this discovery is the four journal questions mentioned earlier. Primarily, the third question is, "What does the

Bible say about what I was wanting?" This question gets not at the surface thing, but at what you were desiring in the inner man when the event happened, as illustrated in the above example.

Another way to help discover what you were after in a crisis event is to add this phrase, "I deserve …" and then add the ending. For example, you might say, "I deserve a break today," "I deserve to have my way," or "I deserve to be first." Then you can begin to unpack what and who you were worshipping when you lost control of yourself and flew into a rage.

This brings us to the next element to consider: what does the righteousness and holiness of God look like? Well, we could begin with the fruit of the Spirit as it is recorded in Galatians 5:22–23a, "love, joy, peace, longsuffering, gentleness, goodness, faith, meekness, temperance."

These would be the first place you need to look when it comes to finding the opposite of whatever idol you are facing. Are you trying to find peace by telling your kids to scram while you are trying to read? There is peace that is a fruit of the Spirit. That comes not by changing your circumstances (having the kids leave your presence), but by developing that relationship with the Lord through reading the Word and praying. Peace might then look like taking the time to enjoy your kids' little circus while you have the time at that moment. They will be gone in just a few minutes anyhow. Then you can go back to your reading. You might just join in their circus and forget about the important reading you were doing.

Another example is someone pulls out in front of you while driving and slows you down. Instead of getting in a rage, you might decide to slow down and take in the scenery more. You exercise self-control by telling yourself the truth, "This person has as much right to the road as I do." It's probable that you do not know the reason this individual pulled in front of you. And because you do not know that reason, but God does, you slow down and thank God for slowing you down. Then the rage does not arise. Instead self-control rises to the top, and you are able to handle the rude driver without becoming angry.

CHAPTER SIX

Putting It All Together

Now that we have an idea of the conduct and the idol of the heart (whatever it is we are worshipping) that has to be put off and the new man that needs to be put on, we must then put the process into practice.

The apostle Paul gave a few examples in the passage following our text that will help you understand this concept. (**Note:** I am only going to use three of the illustrations for this book.)

Lying

Our first illustration has to do with telling lies. In this case, deceit is the primary issue. The text says, "Putting away lying, speak every man truth with his neighbor because we are members of one another" (Eph. 4:25). Deceit is found in all sin. Its root is in the first sin when Satan deceives Eve and prompts her to eat the forbidden fruit. One of the Ten

Commandments also forbids lying. Think about it. Is deceit not present in adultery, murder, covetousness, dishonoring your parents, having other gods, using the Lord's name in vain, and so on?

Think about this. Is there sin in your life where deceit is not present? Clearly we are talking about telling lies. We lie for various reasons, and those motives are the idols of the heart that we pursue. We lie in all kinds of ways:

- with our body language when it is inconsistent with what we are saying
- with our tone of voice when it is inconsistent with what we are saying
- through the use of exaggerations like the words "never" or "always" when they are used to describe someone's actions
- when we hint around or "beat around the bush" when we want something
- when we manipulate to get our way
- even the little white lie

So lying is a problem, most likely, for all of us.

To follow our put-off-and-put-on process you need to discern how and when you use deceit to get what you want. Recently the media revealed that NBC news anchor Brian Williams lied about his coverage of the Iraq War, claiming he had been in a helicopter that enemy ground forces had shot at. Why would he say that if it weren't true?

Without knowing all the facts, but knowing the human heart, it is possible he said that to embellish the intensity of his report and thus give him more credibility because he went through a hair-raising situation. This would fall under the desire for respect or preeminence. In other words, he might have been wanting others to look up to him as a top-notch reporter who was willing to put his life on the line for a story.

Your particular issue might be similar. Some people are the life-of-the-party kind of persons. Others always have something to add. Still others are known as a know-it-all. They deceive themselves and others with their actions and claims because they want to be thought well of or to be liked. Their actions are ways they worship at the idol of self.

Once you have figured out via the journal questions mentioned earlier that lying is a problem, you are ready for the next part, namely renewing the mind. This is where you begin to record and memorize Scripture verses that deal with the issue of deceit. The verse we are dealing with might be one you should memorize, along with the ninth commandment, "Thou shalt not bear false witness." How about Ephesians 4:15, "speaking the truth in love"? You can memorize others to help put off lying.

The next step is to discover what the replacement is for lying. What is the opposite of lying? Well, the text tells us, "speaking the truth." So when you are tempted to lie by embellishing the truth, exaggerating, or telling a bald-faced lie, instead think on the verses you have in your arsenal. Then tell the truth. The more you practice this, the more you will become a truth-teller instead of a liar. So then, not only do you put off the old man and his lies, you are being renewed in your mind, and you are putting on the new man by telling the truth.

Anger

The next verses speak to the issue of anger, "Be ye angry and sin not: Let not the sun go down on your wrath, neither give place to the devil." The text makes it clear that anger is not always sinful. The implication is that it might be sinful to not get angry in a situation. Jesus was angry with the money changers in the temple. We should be angry when we see injustice happen to another person. Certainly there are other occasions when it would be wrong not to be angry.

However, the admonition is that we not sin in our response of anger. Anger is the lack of self-control. So the description of anger would include the use of destructive words or actions in response to a situation in which we become angry. Some of the illustrations I have already used, like road rage, is one of these cases. Yelling, screaming, hitting, throwing things, and so on are ways in which anger is manifested, but so is clamming up and not talking through an issue.

I once had a meeting with a young man at a restaurant to discuss an issue that was close to my heart. I did not know the man, having only met him once or twice. I decided to get there early and see what he did. I had read in the past that it was good to be able to see someone in a setting when he or she does not know you are watching so you can get a measure of this person's heart.

As I saw him drive in, he pulled up to an empty parking space. Another driver arrived from the other direction and saw the same space. My appointment clearly arrived first and should have the spot, but he was having none of the other driver's intrusion. I was close enough to see his face grimace in anger and intimidation at the other driver as he lunged his car forward in a clear attempt to get the other driver to back off. It worked. He got the parking space.

I also got what I wanted. I saw the heart of a man with an anger problem. As I got to know the man over the next few months, my estimation based on that experience in the parking lot proved to be correct.

I have talked enough in the foregoing chapters about anger that you should understand that anger is manifested in many ways (surface issues) for many reasons (under-the-surface issues or idols of the heart). Once you understand how both look in your life, you are ready to put off the old man and be renewed in your mind by memorizing verses and retraining your thinking about your rights. You can then begin to practice self-control as well as redirect (put on the new man) your actions to thanksgiving or like sentiments so you find that you go from being angry to being self-controlled and gentle.

Stealing

The next example is that of a thief. "Let him that stole steal no more: but rather let him labour, working with his hands the thing which is good, that he may have to give to him that needeth" (v. 28).

There are more ways of being a thief than outright robbery. There are those who steal time, identity, reputation, objects, or money, and that is done in multiples of ways. The motive is the same. The victim has something the thief wants and thinks he cannot live without. The process here is the same as the others, put off the outward theft and the inner desire of the heart. The thief is self-centered in focus. He wants something for himself, and he is willing to steal it from someone else in order to obtain it. Perhaps he wants a good reputation before others so he is willing to make another person look bad in comparison to himself. He, in essence, steals the other individual's reputation in order to make his own look better. If thievery is your problem, the key is to consciously put that off and put on its replacement, which we see is to labor for the other person's benefit, "that you may have to give to the one having need."

In other words, if you were in the habit of trying to make yourself look good at the expense of someone else's reputation, then you would reject that notion and replace it with seeking to lift up the other person rather than yourself.

Other examples are in this chapter in Ephesians, but I think enough has been said to enable you to understand the process of put off and put on.

A Case Study

I want to put it all together for you by using a case from my experience that I have flattened out so that no one would be recognized. In fact, it is a few cases put together.

Fred is a middle-aged man who readily admits that he has an anger problem. He told me he had once literally destroyed his kitchen in an angry rant. When he was finished, his cupboards were torn off the walls. The refrigerator was emptied of its contents and lying in a heap in the center of the kitchen, alongside the stove, which he tore away from the wall and destroyed. This is what I would call a major anger problem.

As Fred recounted his upbringing, he told me that his father had an anger problem as well. He and his brothers had to be very careful around their father. Sometimes if they were walking through the kitchen and their father was sitting at the table with a cup of coffee, they had to be ready to run and duck at a moment's notice because their father might fling the coffee mug at them. He could even show me scars on his arms and head where the angry fits of his father had wounded him. Now he was carrying that same kind of behavior into his own life. He wanted out from the bondage to his anger.

The first thing he had to do was to recognize that he had an anger problem. He had already accepted this. He was also very willing to work on it because it had destroyed his marriage and his relationship with his own children.

The second thing he needed to do was learn to recognize when he was prone to outbursts, no matter how slight, even if it were just that inner feeling of being upset that had not been acted on yet. To help him channel the inner feelings of anger, I used the anger journal I spoke of earlier. For one week, I asked him to keep a record of every time he felt mad. He was to answer the four questions:

1. What happened that made him feel angry or get angry?
2. What did he do about it?
3. What did the Bible say about what happened and what he did?
4. What does he need to do now?

His homework was to record, in as much detail as he needed, in order to recall the situation accurately. As for question three, I had given him several verses on anger to read over and to select one to memorize. That would inform him as to what he needed to do now that he had crossed the line into the realm of anger.

After this first week, he came back with his homework in hand. He had several angry events filled out with the questions. With those responses in hand, I could help him see the patterns of behavior that were underlying the angry outbursts. It was obvious that in each case he reacted with angry feelings or outbursts because he was not getting something he wanted. Now the key for him was to begin to think about what it was he wanted so badly that he was willing to get angry in order to have it.

This is where the second set of questions came into play. Like the first collection of questions, I had him answer these for every situation in which he became angry.

1. What happened to precipitate the anger?
2. What was he wanting when he became angry? Notice I didn't ask why he became angry.
3. What does the Bible say about what he was wanting?
4. What does he need to do now?

His responses to these questions helped him think about what he wanted when he became angry. James 4 reminds us we are having conflict because we are wanting something we are not getting, so we fight to get it. In other words, a simple desire we have becomes a demand when we do not obtain it. Thus this leads to anger.

For example, in one of his situations, he felt like he was pressured to talk to his spouse. They had an argument, and he felt he had given a good enough answer to her interrogation. He didn't want to talk about it any longer as they were getting nowhere in his estimation. Instead he told her he didn't want to discuss it now because he needed more time to think about it. He walked away from her, but she kept after him, even grabbing his arm to stop him from walking away.

He turned around, shoved her down, and yelled at her to leave him alone. When he answered the second question about what he was wanting, he said he wanted to be left alone. I helped him to see that he was pursuing peace in his heart. By the way, she was also wanting peace she thought could only be obtained by talking about the problem until she got what she wanted out of the argument. This was only one of the instances.

The pattern seemed to be to him that he was pursuing inner peace in a lot of his situations. When he discovered this and learned when these came up, he began to prepare for them. For example, he found he was most prone to this tendency when he got home from work. He was tired and wanted to just chill out with a drink in his hand after he got home.

His wife, on the other hand, who had been home all day, wanted to talk about the projects she wanted him to finish. He felt pestered, and when she didn't get the response she wanted, she would get mad at him. He, in return, would get mad back. He would sometimes even drive really slowly on the way home because he didn't want to be slammed as soon as he walked in the door. Many times, he would just go to the garage and hang out before going inside.

Now he also found out that his desire for peace was like a weed whose roots grew under the ground and sprouted up in many different places: at work, while driving, or at home around the kids. It seemed that peace was the driving force of his life, and it was as elusive to him as trying to nail Jell-O to the wall. Peace became a hard taskmaster.

Another pattern he learned was that he often became angry when he was made to feel like a loser through failure on the job or by his wife. She often nagged him about those unfinished jobs. In other words, Fred wanted to feel like somebody. When his wife complained about the way he hung their family pictures on the wall, he smashed them on the floor and punched a hole in the wall. In his mind, he couldn't do anything right for her.

He found the same way of thinking showed up at work with his boss or when he was playing ball with his buddies. He would often get upset when he struck out or he missed a play in the field. Rather than go with the flow and learn from the mistake, he would throw a tantrum at the umpire or the boss.

Now that he has recognized some of the patterns in his life, he could begin to look toward how to deal with them in a way that pleased God. Fred recognized his under-the-surface idol was peace and to look good to others—pride. He also recognized where and when those idols popped up in his path. Thus, he was able to make the following plan in preparation for those potholes in his life.

Whenever he was playing ball with his buddies, he would pray for strength from the Lord to control himself. Secondly, he went over some proverbs on anger, such as Proverbs 25:28 (ESV), "A man without self control is like a city broken into and left without walls." He reminded himself that a city in that culture was vulnerable to destruction by outside forces. When he became angry, he was like that. So he prayed not to be like that. Each time he took the field or stepped up to the plate, he would pray for God to enable him to handle himself in a godly fashion. If he didn't perform as he wanted to, he would tell himself he did his best and even commend the pitcher in his mind or verbally if he struck out. If he failed and became angry, he would confess his sin to those around him who witnessed his outbursts or were the brunt of his anger as well as to God, and he would ask for forgiveness.

His plan with his wife was to prepare himself as he went home by repeating a verse of Scripture like Ephesians 5:25, "Husbands love your wives as Christ also loved the church and gave himself for it." Then he would thank God for his wife and all her hard work she put in at home. He would walk in and talk to her until she was done telling him what had happened in her day or whatever she wanted to talk about. He also kept a list of things that needed to be done around the house and began to check them off. He did the best he could with the tasks she asked him to do. Again, if there were failures on his part, he would ask forgiveness from her and God. In time, she began to see a change in him, and she began to ease up on her demands of him.

Conclusion

I hope this short book has helped you to identify the sinful habits you practice on a daily basis. I hope it will put you on the path to discovery and how to find freedom from the bondage you feel as a result of those sins. You have been equipped to put off those sinful habits, be changed in your thinking, and put on the new man that God has created you to be.

Don't just lay aside this book and forget about what you have read. Read through these final questions and begin the put-off-and-put-on process in your own life.

1. What is the most pressing sinful habit you have? Write it down.
2. Use the two sets of four journal questions (Appendix A and B) for at least one week, and then identify the patterns of conduct as to when and where your sin pops up and what you were wanting.
3. Find in the Bible as many verses as you can that address your sinful habits. Use a topical Bible index or a concordance, or talk to me, your pastor, or counselor for help in finding verses that address your issue.

4. Confess and repent of your sin.
5. Write out a plan to put off/mortify your sin, be renewed in the spirit of your mind (change your thinking), and put on what is the new man (the right thinking and action).
6. Thank God for the transformation that is taking place in you.

It has been a blessing to me to write this book in order to equip you to grow spiritually, but I cannot do this for you. You must take it upon yourself and step out in obedience. God will bless you for it. Your family will bless you for it. Your friends and coworkers will bless you for it. I bless you for it.

> The Lord bless you and keep you: The Lord make His face shine upon you and be gracious to you: The Lord lift up His countenance upon you and give you peace (Num. 6:24–26)(ESV).

Appendix A

1. What happened?
   a. *Write down information describing the situation that led to the failure. The key is to not try to write everything down, but enough so you can recall what happened.*

2. What did I do?
   a. *What was my response to what happened?*

3. What should I have done in response to what happened?
    a. *What did God want me to do? Of course the answer comes from the Scripture.*

4. What do I need to do now?
    a. *What does the Scripture say I need to do to correct the situation?*

Appendix B

1. What happened?
   a. *This is similar to the first set of questions.*

2. What was I wanting when the event happened?

3. What does the Bible say about what I was wanting?

4. What do I need to do now?

Printed in the United States
By Bookmasters